Places We Live

Living Beside a
River

Ellen Labrecque

raintree

Raintree is an imprint of Capstone Global Library Limited, a company incorporated in England and Wales
having its registered office at 7 Pilgrim Street, London, EC4V 6LB – Registered company number: 6695582

www.raintree.co.uk
myorders@raintree.co.uk

Edited by James Benefield and Brenda Haugen
Designed by Richard Parker
Original illustrations © Capstone Global Library 2015
Picture research by Jo Miller
Production by Helen McCreath
Originated by Capstone Global Library Ltd
Printed and bound in China

ISBN 978 1 406 28774 5 (hardback)
18 17 16 15 14
10 9 8 7 6 5 4 3 2 1

ISBN 978 1 406 28781 3 (paperback)
19 18 17 16 15
10 9 8 7 6 5 4 3 2 1

British Library Cataloguing in Publication Data
A full catalogue record for this book is available from the British Library.

Acknowledgments
We would like to thank the following for permission to reproduce photographs: Alamy: Paul Springett
C, 25; AP Images: Kusumadireza, 26; Corbis: Tiziana and Gianni Baldizzone, 5; Getty Images: National
Geographic/Timothy G. Laman, 19, The Image Bank/Zigy Kaluzny-Charles Thatcher, 21; Newscom: Andre
Jenny Stock Connection Worldwide, 14, Danita Delimont Photography/David Wall, 4, Danita Delimont
Photography/Pete Oxford, 13, imago stock & people, 27; Shutterstock: Alexander A. Trofimov, 20, alice-
photo, 12, Dan Schreiber, 10, dimbar76, cover, Dobresum, 9, EpicStockMedia, 24, Frontpage, 6, Grisha
Bruev, 18, Lisa-Lisa, 16, Lukasz Janyst, 11, maigi, 15, Neale Cousland, 22, Peter Stuckings, 8, Ritu Manoj
Jethani, 17, Strahil Dimitrov, 23.

Design Elements: Shutterstock: donatas1205, Olympus.

We would like to thank Rachel Bowles for her invaluable help in the preparation of this book.

Contents

Some words are shown in bold, **like this**. You can find
out what they mean by looking in the glossary.

What is a river?

Rivers are large natural streams of running water. They can start as **springs**, lakes and **glaciers**. Rivers make **channels** and flow into other lakes or rivers. They end in a mouth, which flows into the sea often through an **estuary** or a **delta**.

A mouth of a river is where a river "ends" and meets the sea or ocean.

People live by rivers because they are useful in many ways.

Animals, plants and people cannot live without water, so rivers can be great places to live! Living by a river means you can easily travel, move things around, fish and farm.

Where are rivers?

Rivers are found on every **continent** and on all types of land. They begin on mountains or hills. Here, rainwater or water from melted snow collects and forms streams. As the stream collects more water, it forms a river.

The River Nile flows through 10 countries and ends in the Mediterranean Sea.

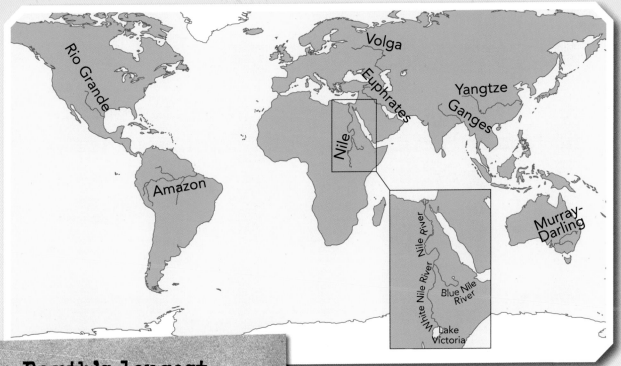

Earth's longest rivers

1. River Nile, Africa: 6,650 kilometres (4,132 miles)

2. Amazon River, South America: 6,400 kilometres (3,976 miles)

3. Yangtze River, China: 6,300 kilometres (3,915 miles)

4. Mississippi–Missouri river system, USA: 3,766 kilometres (2,340 miles)

The River Nile has several **sources** which mostly flow into Lake Victoria. On the north end of Lake Victoria, water pours over a waterfall. This is Ripon Falls. It pours into a narrow opening and this is where the Nile really begins.

Rivers of the past

Rivers have helped shape our land over time. Scientists think the Colorado River, in Arizona, United States, eroded the rock to make the Grand Canyon.

Scientists think it took the Colorado River millions of years to carve the Grand Canyon.

The Amazon River still attracts explorers – some of whom are tourists.

People in the past have followed river paths to explore new parts of the world. Explorers sailed down rivers to discover new parts of Africa, and North and South America. There are now cities in some of these places.

Living beside a river

One of the main reasons people live in **settlements** by a river is food. Rivers create perfect land beside them for growing **crops**. The river also gives farmers water for watering their plants.

Land by a river is usually fertile. This means it is good to grow crops there.

New York City is able to ship goods all over the world using two rivers.

People live by rivers in villages, towns and cities. Some people even live in floating homes. The biggest city in the United States, New York City, has the Hudson River on one side and the East River on the other.

All kinds of people

Cities grow around rivers because of **trade**. This started when people bought and sold things such as spices, tea and sugar. People could travel down rivers and trade from country to country. Trade still happens today.

Over 8 million people live in London which is built beside the River Thames. London increased in size because of trade happening there.

The Tagaeri people drink water from the river.

There are not many cities or towns along the Amazon River in South America. There are mostly rainforests. The Tagaeri people live here as nomads. They don't stay in one place but instead travel to find food.

Flooding rivers

The biggest problem with living beside a river is the danger of flooding. Rivers flood when they get too much water from rainfall or melting snow. This makes the water level rise over the **riverbanks**.

A flood can increase river levels by 100 times its normal flow.

Some houses along rivers are built on stilts to keep them dry.

Overflowing river water can destroy anything in its path. It can also drown people. Walls and barriers called floodwalls are built around rivers to stop floods. The Mississippi River in the United States has raised banks called levees.

Canal living

Rivers are so useful we have built our own! Canals are dug-out **trenches** that are filled with water. They are made so boats can move things from the sea to places inland.

Canals were useful to move goods before there were railways. But today there are still canals being used for trade.

You can only get around Venice on foot or on boats, such as these gondolas.

Venice, Italy, is famous for its canals. It is one of the only cities in the world that has almost no cars. Over 100 canals go through the city and empty into the Adriatic Sea.

Getting around

People use rivers to move from one place to another. If the river is wide enough, you can sail giant ships down rivers. Some people paddle on rivers in canoes, kayaks or small rafts.

Many people holiday on cruise ships that leave from river ports.

The Staten Island ferry ride is 8 kilometres (5 miles) long and takes 25 minutes each way.

Some people use river ferries to travel to work. In the East River, near New York City, the Staten Island Ferry takes 60,000 passengers a day between Staten Island and the city.

Riverbank and plant life

We eat a lot of the plant and animal life that live in and near rivers. For example, rivers are great places to catch fish. Many plants, such as reeds and bullrushes, grow in the soil by rivers.

There is plenty of food for fish in rivers so there are lots of fish.

Mud found near rivers can be used as building material for homes.

We find materials such as straw, clay and mud by rivers. We can use these materials for building. Some people collect river rocks to build paths in their gardens!

What is work like?

You can be a teacher, nurse or writer and live by a river. But living by a river also offers special jobs. For example, rivers can be popular with tourists. Tourists love everything from watersports to seeing the sights.

Riverside attractions, such as this fort, need people to help run them.

River engineers can change the direction the water flows in a river.

Some people work by rivers. River engineers study rivers to try and stop flooding and stop **pollution**. Many rivers have large and small ship building yards, providing many different types of jobs.

Fun things to do

People visit rivers because they offer many fun things to do. You can swim, fish and water-ski in rivers. Some of the most popular things to do on a river are kayaking, canoeing or white water rafting.

River sports can be thrilling but also dangerous.

Only expert paddlers tackle the roughest rivers.

Rivers are graded so you can tell how rough the river is. There are six levels or grades. The lowest, Grade 1, means the river is calm and safe. Grade 6 means it is dangerous.

Rivers of the future

Many rivers today are polluted. The waste comes from cities and factories dumping their rubbish. Sometimes rivers are **overfished**, too. This leaves people and animals without enough food.

Water **pollution** kills plant and animal life.

Since 1998, the Living Lands group has picked up over 15 million kilograms (7 million pounds) of river rubbish. Other groups have planted new trees along **riverbanks**. For example, these can give animals food and places to live.

Fun facts

- Long ago, people found gold in rivers such as the Klondike River in Canada.

- The River Volga in Russia is frozen solid for around three months of the year.

- Eleven of Russia's 20 biggest cities are next to one river, the River Volga.

- Races in kayaks and canoes in the summer Olympics can take place on rivers.

- Seventy-six rivers in the world are over 1,609 kilometres (1,000 miles) long.

- China has a number of the longest rivers in the world running through it. These include the Yangtze River and the Yellow River.

- Most of the world's major cities sit on a river.

Quiz

Which of the following sentences are true? Which are false?

1. Rivers are only found on some continents.

2. Canals are waterways that are man-made.

3. Some people travel to work on rivers.

4. People discovered new places in the world by following rivers.

5. All the rivers around the world are clean.

1. Fals. Rivers are found on all continents.

2. True. Canals are trenches built by people.

3. True. People travel to work on rivers every day.

4. True. Explorers followed rivers to find new places.

5. False. Some rivers are badly polluted. Some people work to clean them up.

Glossary

channel passage through which a river flows

continent any of the world's seven biggest land masses: Africa; Antarctica; Asia; Australia; Europe; North America; South America

crops plants grown by people for food

delta triangle-shaped piece of land at the mouth of the river where it flows into an ocean, sea or lake

eroded when land or rock has been worn or ground down over time by water, ice, snow or wind

estuary where a river meets the sea; it is salty and has tides

glacier slow-moving icy mass or river of ice

overfish when people have taken too many fish from a river, sea or lake

pollution rubbish, waste, sand and mud that makes the air, land, rivers or seas dirty and unsafe

riverbank land along a river

settlement place where people live for good, such as a village, town or city

spring place where rivers can start when underground water reaches the surface

source place where a river starts

trade when you buy and sell things

trenches long, narrow ditches. These can be dug by people, or they can exist in nature.

Find out more

Books

Pond and River, Steve Parker (DK Eyewitness Books, 2011)

Rivers (Habitat Survival), Melanie Waldron (Raintree, 2012)

The World's Most Amazing Rivers, Anita Ganeri (Raintree, 2009)

Websites

www.bbc.co.uk/schools/riversandcoasts

Find out more about rivers and coasts on this BBC site.

http://education.nationalgeographic.com/education/encyclopedia/river/?ar_a=5
This National Geographic website has lots of river facts and information.

www.internationalrivers.org

This site helps us learn how we can keep our rivers clean and healthy.

www.primaryhomeworkhelp.co.uk/rivers.html
This is a great site to visit if you need help with homework about rivers.

Index